NUMBER TRACING

This book belongs to

_____

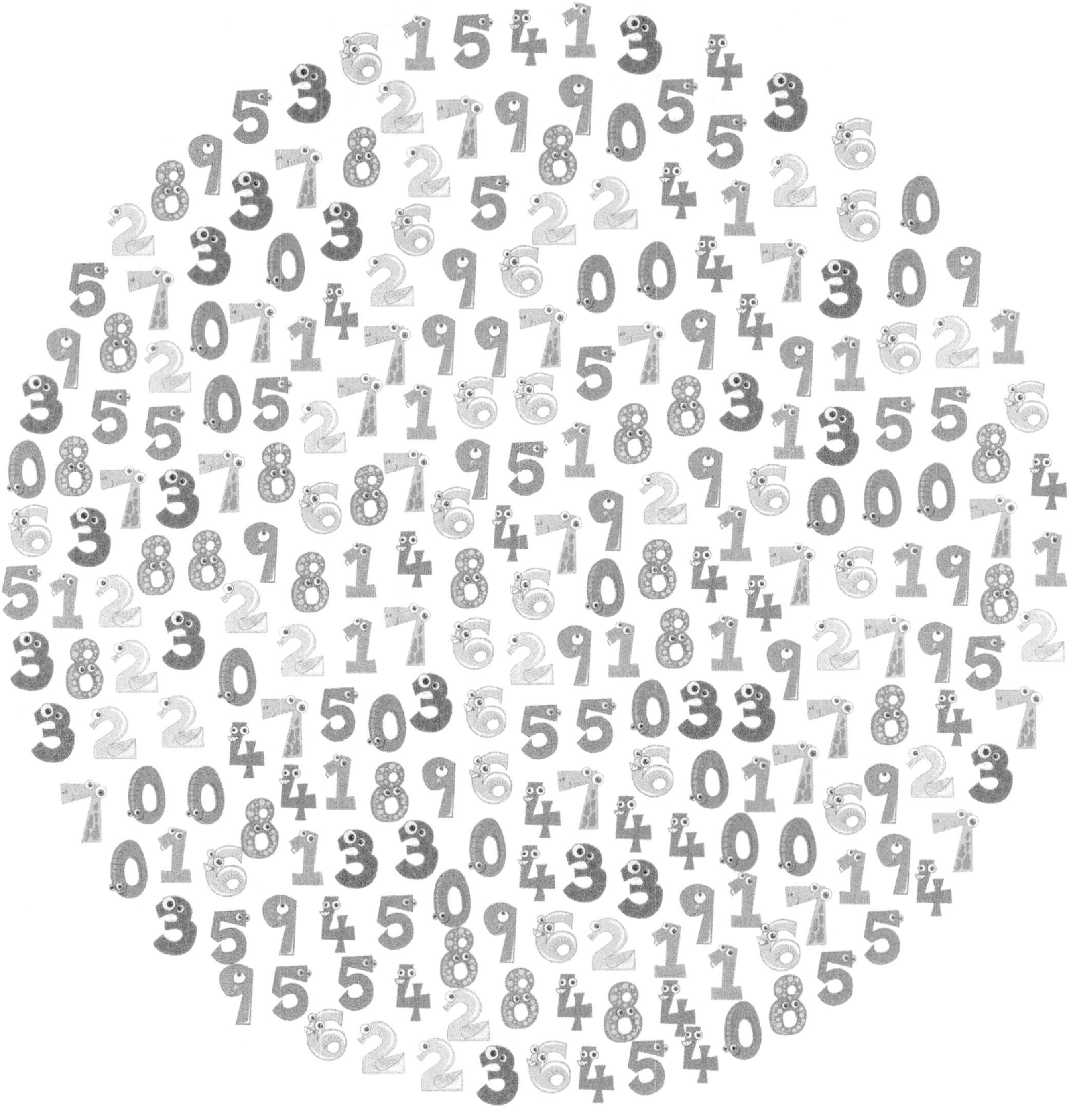

I have ___1___ robot

one

1 2 3 4 5 6 7 8 9 10 11 12 13 14 15 16 17 18 19 20

Let's write 1

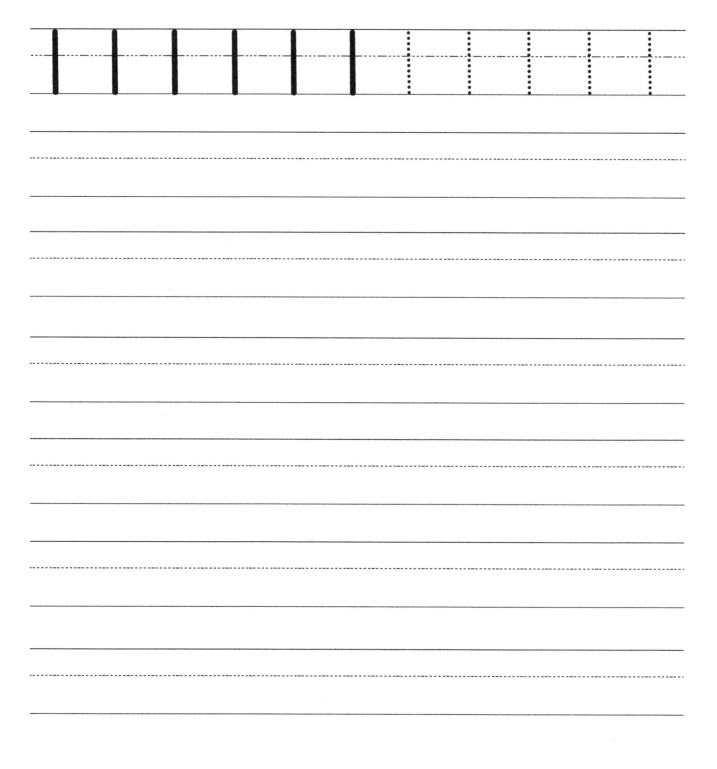

1 2 3 4 5 6 7 8 9 10 11 12 13 14 15 16 17 18 19 20

one one one one

Do you remember?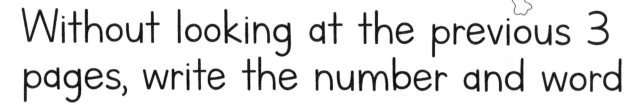

Without looking at the previous 3 pages, write the number and word

number

word

AWESOME WORK - YOU ARE A ★

I have 2 dinosaurs

two

Let's write 2

2 2 2 2 2 2 2 2

two two two two

Do you remember?

Without looking at the previous 3 pages, write the number and word

number

word

1 2 **3** 4 5 6 7 8 9 10 11 12 13 14 15 16 17 18 19 20

I have 3 planes

three

Let's write 3

3 3 3 3 3 3 3 3

three

three three three

Do you remember?

Without looking at the previous 3 pages, write the number and word

| number |

| word |

THERE'S NO STOPPING YOU NOW!

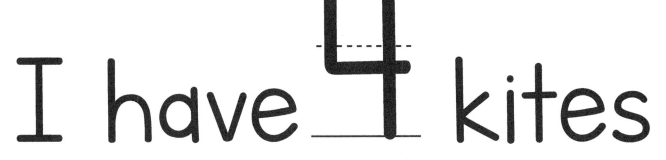

I have 4 kites

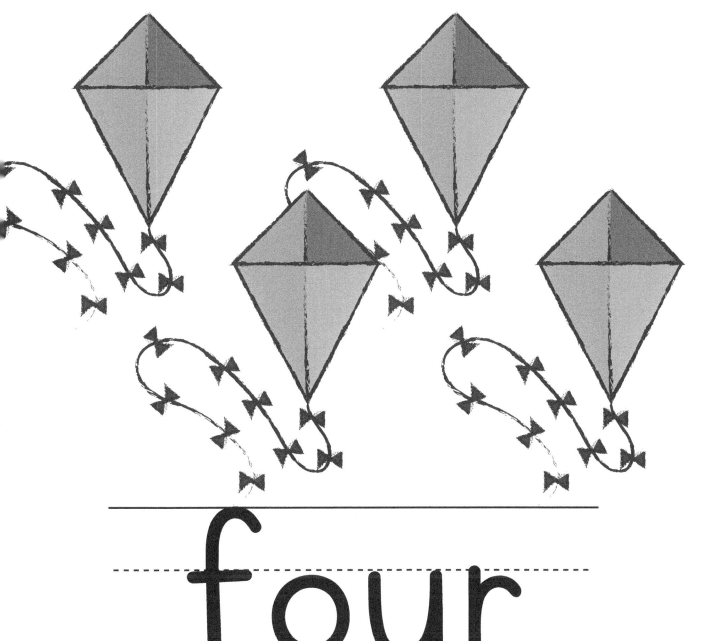

four

Let's write 4

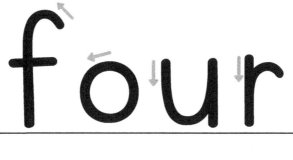

four four four four

Do you remember?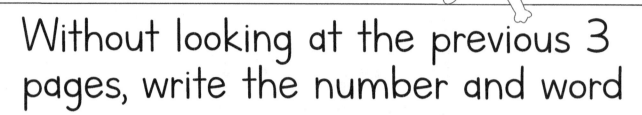

Without looking at the previous 3 pages, write the number and word

number	

word	

YOU JUST GET BETTER AND BETTER

1 2 3 4 **5** 6 7 8 9 10 11 12 13 14 15 16 17 18 19 20

I have 5 bunnies

five

Let's write 5

5 5 5 5 5 5 5 5

five five five five

Do you remember?

Without looking at the previous 3 pages, write the number and word

number

word

I have 6 trees

six

Let's write 6

6 6 6 6 6 6 6 6

six

six six six six six six

Do you remember?

Without looking at the previous 3 pages, write the number and word

| number |

| word |

7

I have 7 apples

seven

Let's write 7 →

7 7 7 7 7 7 7 7 7

1 2 3 4 5 6 **7** 8 9 10 11 12 13 14 15 16 17 18 19 20

seven

seven seven seven

Do you remember?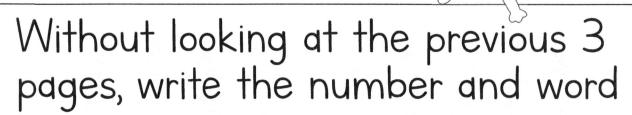

Without looking at the previous 3 pages, write the number and word

| number |
| word |

YOU TOTALLY ACED THAT!

1 2 3 4 5 6 7 **8** 9 10 11 12 13 14 15 16 17 18 19 20

I have 8 owls

eight

Let's write 8

8 8 8 8 8 8 8 8

eight

eight   eight   eight

Do you remember?

Without looking at the previous 3 pages, write the number and word

| number |

| word |

1 2 3 4 5 6 7 8 **9** 10 11 12 13 14 15 16 17 18 19 20

I have **9** pencils

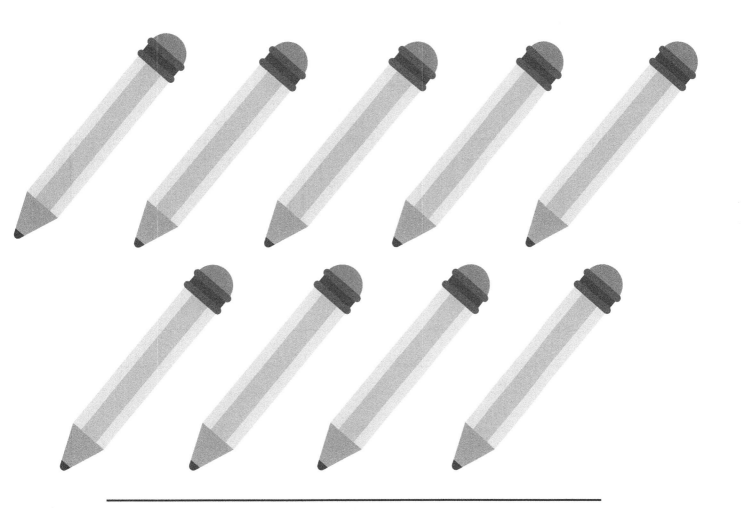

nine

Let's write 9

9 9 9 9 9 9 9 9 9

nine

nine nine nine nine

Do you remember?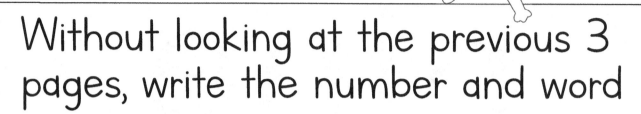

Without looking at the previous 3 pages, write the number and word

number

word

YOU'RE ONE SMART COOKIE

I have 10 books

ten

Let's write 10

ten ten ten ten ten

Do you remember?

Without looking at the previous 3 pages, write the number and word

number

word

1 2 3 4 5 6 7 8 9 10 **11** 12 13 14 15 16 17 18 19 20

I have 11 chimps

eleven

1 2 3 4 5 6 7 8 9 10 **11** 12 13 14 15 16 17 18 19 20

Let's write 11

eleven

eleven eleven eleven

Do you remember?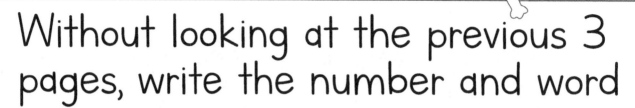

Without looking at the previous 3 pages, write the number and word

number

word

BRAINS AS WELL AS GOOD LOOKS! 😉

1 2 3 4 5 6 7 8 9 10 11 **12** 13 14 15 16 17 18 19 20

I have 12 balls

twelve

1 2 3 4 5 6 7 8 9 10 11 **12** 13 14 15 16 17 18 19 20

Let's write 12

12 12 12 12 12 12 12

twelve

twelve twelve twelve

Do you remember?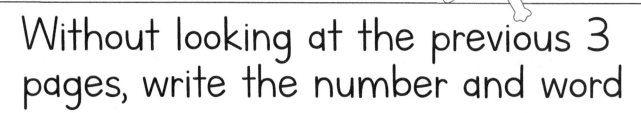

Without looking at the previous 3 pages, write the number and word

number

word

I have 13 cats

thirteen

Let's write 13

13 13 13 13 13 13 13

1 2 3 4 5 6 7 8 9 10 11 12 **13** 14 15 16 17 18 19 20

thirteen

thirteen thirteen

Do you remember?

Without looking at the previous 3 pages, write the number and word

number

word

HAIL TO THE NUMBER HERO

I have 14 balloons

fourteen

Let's write 14

fourteen

fourteen fourteen

Do you remember?

number	

word	

EVEN SANTA IS IMPRESSED

I have 15 drums

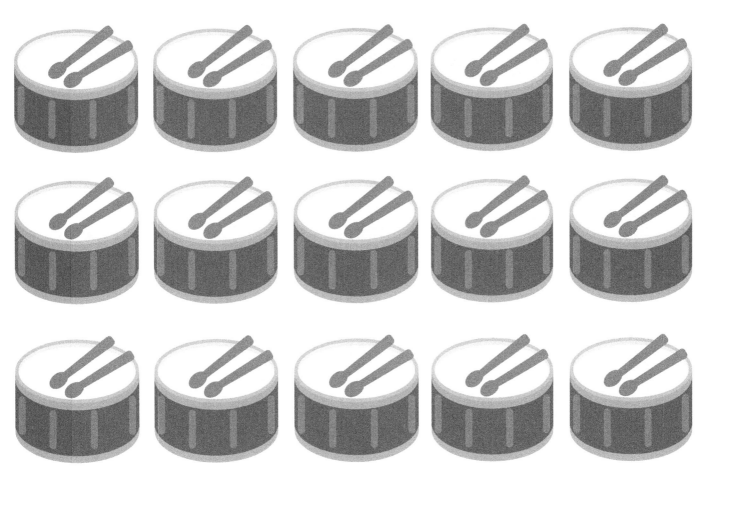

fifteen

Let's write 15

15 15 15 15 15 15 15

fifteen

fifteen fifteen fifteen

Do you remember?

Without looking at the previous 3 pages, write the number and word

number

word

YOU TOTALLY ROCK!

1 2 3 4 5 6 7 8 9 10 11 12 13 14 15 **16** 17 18 19 20

I have 16 pandas

sixteen

Let's write 16

16 16 16 16 16 16 16

sixteen

sixteen sixteen sixteen

Do you remember?
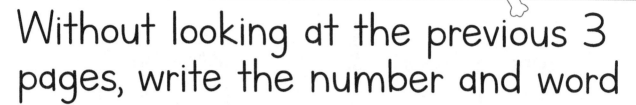

Without looking at the previous 3 pages, write the number and word

number

word

I have 17 guitars

seventeen

Let's write 17

17 17 17 17 17 17 17 17

seventeen

seventeen seventeen

Do you remember?

Without looking at the previous 3 pages, write the number and word

number

word

I have 18 lions

eighteen

1 2 3 4 5 6 7 8 9 10 11 12 13 14 15 16 17 **18** 19 20

Let's write 18

18 18 18 18 18 18 18

eighteen

eighteen eighteen

Do you remember?

Without looking at the previous 3 pages, write the number and word

number

word

YOU'RE ON FIRE

I have 19 fish

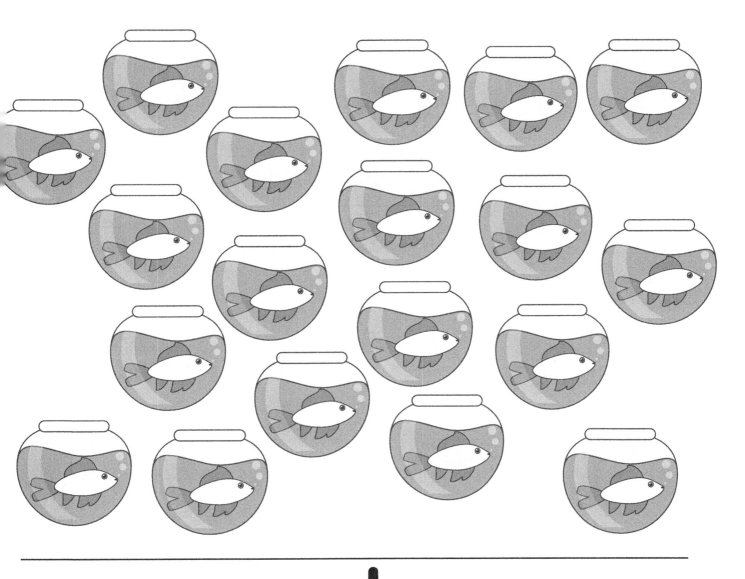

nineteen

Let's write 19

19 19 19 19 19 19 19 19

nineteen

nineteen nineteen

Do you remember?

Without looking at the previous 3 pages, write the number and word

number

word

THAT'S ONE CLEVER KID

I have 20 dogs

twenty

Let's write 20

20 20 20 20 20 20

twenty

twenty twenty twenty

Do you remember?

Without looking at the previous 3 pages, write the number and word

number

word

AWESOME WORK!

You have done brilliantly with your number writing - we couldn't be more proud of you!

Give yourself a huge pat on the back and ask mom or dad for a special treat - tell them the book said they had to!

EASY MATH

We are mightily impressed with how well you've done so far.

In fact, you're so good we think you can easily do some simple math.

Let's start with addition . . .

Easy Addition

Addition is bringing two or more numbers (or things) together to make a new total

$$1 + 2 = 3$$

o   oo   ooo

Here, 1 circle is added to 2 other circles to make a total of 3 circles

Let's look at a few more examples . . .

Easy Addition

$1 + 3 = 4$

o   ooo   ooo o

$2 + 1 = 3$

oo   o   ooo

$3 + 2 = 5$

ooo   oo   ooo oo

Easy Addition

1 + 4 = 5

6 + 3 = 9

Now you try ➡

Easy Addition

1 + 1 = ☐

2 + 1 = ☐

3 + 2 = ☐

Easy Addition

4 + 2 = ☐
○○○
○

2 + ○○

○○○
○○○

2 + 2 = ☐
○○ ○○

○○○
○

3 + 3 = ☐
○○○ ○○○

○○○
○○○

Easy Addition

Let's take away the circles

$2 + 1 =$ ☐

$4 + 1 =$ ☐

$3 + 2 =$ ☐

Easy Addition

Let's take away the circles

$3 + 3 = \boxed{}$

$4 + 2 = \boxed{}$

$3 + 4 = \boxed{}$

Easy Addition

Let's take away the circles

$3 + 5 = $ ☐

$5 + 4 = $ ☐

$4 + 4 = $ ☐

Easy Addition

These ones are tough!

$6 + 5 =$ ☐

$7 + 6 =$ ☐

$8 + 3 =$ ☐

Easy Addition

These are super tough!

$8 + 12 = \boxed{}$

$10 + 11 = \boxed{}$

$12 + 9 = \boxed{}$

Easy Subtraction

Subtraction is the opposite of addition. You take one number away from another

$$3 - 2 = 1$$

Here, we start with 3 circles and then take 2 away, which leaves us with just 1 circle

Let's look at a few more examples . . .

Easy Subtraction

2 - 1 = 1

3 - 1 = 2

4 - 2 = 2

Easy Subtraction

5 - 2 = 3

○○○
○○

○○

○○○

6 - 3 = 3

○○○
○○○

○○○

○○○

Now you try ➡

Easy Subtraction

2 - 1 = ☐

3 - 2 = ☐

4 - 2 = ☐

Easy Subtraction

5 - 1 =

6 - 3 =

6 - 5 =

Easy Subtraction

Let's take away the circles

$3 - 1 =$ ☐

$4 - 3 =$ ☐

$5 - 1 =$ ☐

Easy Subtraction

Let's take away the circles

6 - 3 = ☐

7 - 5 = ☐

8 - 2 = ☐

Easy Subtraction

Let's take away the circles

9 - 5 = ☐

7 - 4 = ☐

6 - 2 = ☐

Easy Subtraction

These ones are tough!

10 - 4 = ☐

12 - 3 = ☐

14 - 7 = ☐

Easy Subtraction

These are super tough!

12 − 11 = ☐

15 − 12 = ☐

18 − 14 = ☐

Do you remember?

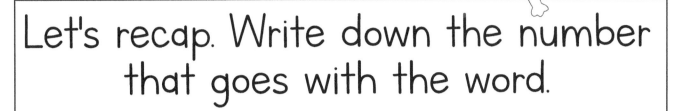

Let's recap. Write down the number that goes with the word.

Eighteen	Two
Twelve	Six
One	Seventeen

Do you remember?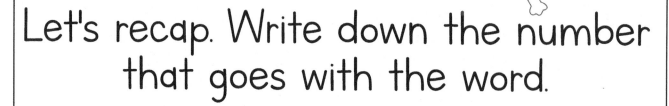

Let's recap. Write down the number that goes with the word.

Twenty	Fourteen
Five	Seven
Nineteen	Three

Sixteen	Eight
Four	Thirteen
Nine	Fifteen
Eleven	Ten

You are Number 1 in our book for reaching the end!

Keep learning, keep exploring